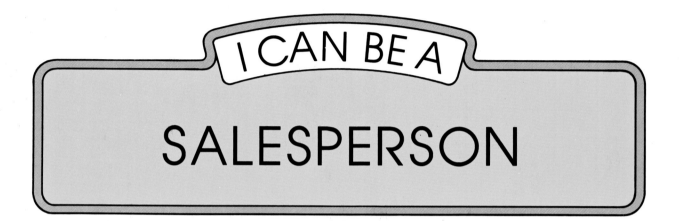

I CAN BE A

SALESPERSON

By Carol Greene

Prepared under the direction of Robert L. Hillerich, Ph.D.

ℂℙ CHILDRENS PRESS®
CHICAGO

Library of Congress Cataloging—in—Publication Data

Greene, Carol.
   I can be a salesperson / by Carol Greene.
     p. cm.
   Includes index.
   Summary: Describes the work of different types of sales
people and the kinds of things they sell.
   ISBN 0-516-01959-7
   1. Sales personnel—Juvenile literature. 2. Selling—Juvenile
literature. 3. Retail trade—Juvenile literature. (1. Sales
personnel. 2. Selling. 3. Occupations.) I. Title.
HF5439.5.G74 1989
658.8'5'02373—dc20

89-15848
CIP
AC

Childrens Press®, Chicago
Copyright ©1989 by Regensteiner Publishing Enterprises, Inc.
All rights served. Published simultaneously in Canada.
Printed in the United States of America.
1 2 3 4 5 6 7 8 9 10 R 98 97 96 95 94 93 92 91 90 89

This book is for Jim Graham.

PICTURE DICTIONARY

customer

order

store

goods

salespeople

peddler

barter

"Hot cross buns!"

"Who will buy my strawberries?"

"Get your evening paper!"

People have been selling for thousands of years. Some sell on street corners. Some sell in stores. Some use telephones or travel from place to place.

barter

peddler

Before there was money, people traded one thing for another. They traded fish for furs or maybe a cooking pot for some meat. This is called bartering.

Early settlers often lived far from towns. Peddlers came to their homes. They sold many different things—pots and pans, cloth, thread, and tools.

Long ago, salespeople sold their goods in open-air markets much like this one in London, England. Today, some salespeople work in stores and others visit their customers. But there are still some who sell in markets like this.

This food route salesman (above) drives around to grocery stores, delivers food, takes orders for more food, and gives the store owner a bill. The salespeople on the opposite page are selling shoes, computers, pretzels, and airplanes.

salespeople

goods

Salespeople still sell many different things. Some sell goods. Shoes, airplanes, cat food, computers, and teddy bears are all goods.

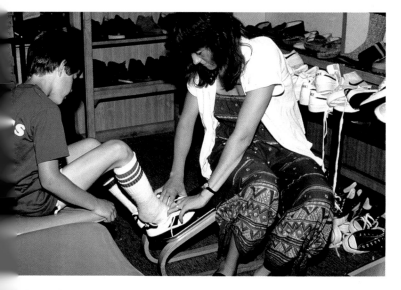

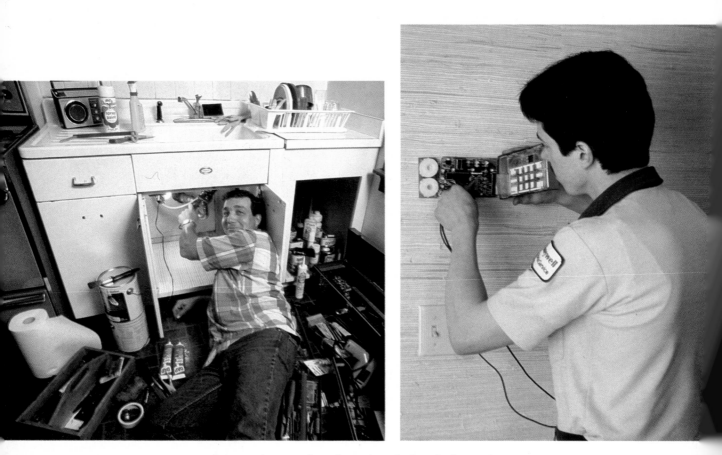

Some salespeople sell services instead of goods.
These services might include plumbing or installing
home alarm systems (above). Some other services
are teaching dancing lessons, renting cars, and
cleaning rugs (opposite page).

Other salespeople sell
services. Home repairs are
a service. So are dancing
lessons and rug cleaning.

At a trade show (above), salespeople from many different companies show their products. Below left, a sales representative explains a piece of equipment to a sausage company manager. Below right, a sales representative from a clothing manufacturer shows dresses to the buyer from a department store.

Many salespeople work for companies. The companies make the products that they sell. These salespeople are called sales representatives.

Some sales representatives sell their goods to other companies. One sells special trucks to factories. Another sells heart machines to hospitals. Yet another sells books to schools and libraries.

Other sales
representatives sell to
stores. One might sell
sports equipment. Another
might sell toys.

Some sales representatives try anything
to draw attention to their products.

Sales representatives must travel. Good ones may be put in charge of a whole district. Someday they may go back and work in their company's marketing division.

Left: A salesperson helps a boy try on some camping equipment.
Right: A salesperson tells a customer about a refrigerator
he may want to buy.

store

Many other salespeople work in stores. They might start by selling clothes or furniture. If they are good, they could be put in

Left: This record store manager began as a salesperson.
Top right: A store manager watches a salesperson write up a bill.
Bottom right: A market manager telephones an order to a salesperson.

charge of a department.

Some end up as manager

of a whole store or even

a group of stores.

Left: An insurance agent meets with a couple in their home.
Right: Using a listing book, a real estate agent looks up houses for sale.
Opposite page: A customer visits a house she may want to buy.

Salespeople work in
many different ways. Real
estate agents help people
buy and sell houses.
Insurance agents make
their sales in people's
homes.

Left: Clothing store salesperson who earns a commission
Right: Man in wheelchair making telephone sales

Some salespeople earn
a salary for doing their
job. But many work on
commission. This means
they get paid part of the
price of each thing they sell.

20

Above left: Selling food from an outdoor cart
Above right: Selling balloons in the park
Below: Selling smoke alarms to home owners

Left: A salesperson checks a list of products for a customer.
Above: A salesperson from a fabric factory shows boards full of samples to a customer.

customer

Often salespeople must hunt for the right customers. They must decide which product is best for each customer.

Then they show or explain the product in an interesting way. They help

Left: This Girl Scout has convinced a customer that she would like to buy some cookies.
Above: Salesperson writing up an order for some picture frames

the customer see what a good product it is.

At last they ask the customer to buy the product. If the customer says yes, they write up an order.

order

All this means that
salespeople must get
along with others. They
must like and understand
people.

They must also
understand the products
they are selling. It is

important that they like
the products, too.

Salespeople should
know how to speak well.
They should be able to
write good letters. And
they *must* be good at
arithmetic.

Sometimes salespeople
do a lot of things in one
day. They drive or fly.
They meet with customers.
They stop in at their
office. They must be able
to use their time well.

Salespeople who smile can sell more.

Many salespeople earn
a good living. But even
the best ones go through
bad times. So a good
salesperson should know
how to smile and try
again—and again.

There are salespeople of all ages.

Salespeople can be young or old. They can be women or men. Some go to college. Some do not. Many stores put new salespeople through their own training program.

But the best jobs almost always go to college graduates. These people often study business. Sometimes they must learn about special fields, such as music, education, or medicine.

Do you like to meet many kinds of people? Can you charm the rattles off a snake? Are you full of bounce and drive?

Then you can be a salesperson!

WORDS YOU SHOULD KNOW

barter (BAR • ter)—to trade one thing for another

commission (kuh • MISH • un)—part of the price of each thing sold that is paid to the salesperson

customer (KUS • tuh • mer)—a person who might buy something

department (de • PART • ment)—one section of a store

district (DIS • trikt)—one section of the country

goods (GOODZ)—items that can be seen and touched

insurance agent (in • SHUR • ans AY • jent)—a person who sells insurance

manager (MAN • i • jer)—a person in charge of something

marketing division (MAR • ket • ing di • VEE • zhun)—the part of a company that works with selling

order (OR • der)—a statement that says that a customer wants to buy a certain thing

peddler (PED • ler)—a person who travels around with things to sell

product (PRAH • dukt)—something that is made

real estate agent (REEL es • TAYT AY • jent)—a person who helps people buy and sell houses

salary (SAL • a • ree)—a regular amount of money paid to someone for doing a job

sales representative (SAYLZ rep • ree • ZENT • a • tiv)—a person who sells the products that a company makes

services (SER • vi • siz)—things that people do for other people

store (STOR)—a place where customers come to buy things

training program (TRAY • ning PRO • gram)—information about doing a job

INDEX

PHOTO CREDITS
Cameramann International, Ltd.—4, 7 (3 photos), 8, 9 (upper right), 11 (lower left), 12, 16 (right), 17 (top right), 17 (bottom right), 19, 22, 23, 24 (left)
© Brent Jones—4 (upper right), 14, 15, 17 (left), 22 (left), 25 (right), 26 (right)
Journalism Services:
  © Melanie Carr—18 (left)
© Norma Morrison—16 (left), 20 (right), 24 (right), 25 (right)
Root Resources:
  © Don and Pat Valenti—4, 9 (upper right), 9 (lower right), 21 (bottom), 28 (right)
  © Ray Hillstrom—12 (top)
TSW/Click Chicago:
  © Donovan Reese—9 (lower left)
Third Coast Stock Source:
  © Paul H. Henning—10 (left)
  © Scott Witte—10 (right), 12 (lower right)
  © Lawrence Ruggeri—11 (top)
  © Alan R. Bagg—11 (bottom right)
  © Eric Oxendorf—21 (top)
  © Ken Osburn—26 (left)
  © Bob Clarke—27
  © John Touscany—28 (left)
  © Buck Miller—Cover
Karen Yops—4 (middle right, lower left), 18 (right), 20 (left), 21 (top right), 23 (right)

ABOUT THE AUTHOR

Carol Greene has degrees in English literature and musicology. She has worked in international exchange programs, as an editor, and as a teacher. She now lives in St. Louis, Missouri, and writes full time. She has published over seventy books for children. Others in this series include *I Can Be a Football Player, I Can Be a Baseball Player, I Can Be a Model, I Can Be a Librarian,* and *I Can Be a Forest Ranger.*